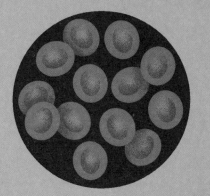
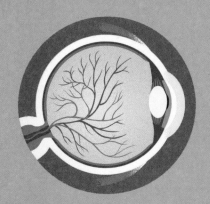

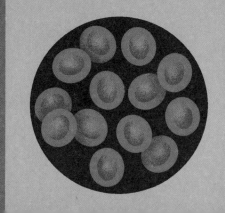
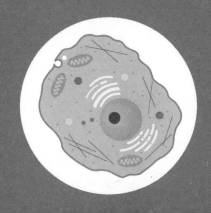
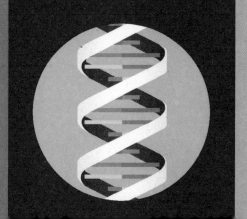
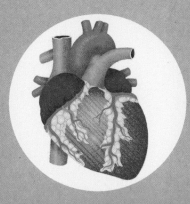

BEN NEWMAN

Dedicated to our biological marvel,
Wilbur Franklin Newman, who was born
during the making of this book.

DR. DOMINIC WALLIMAN

Dedicated to the little
chaps Leon and Harrison.

Every attempt has been made to ensure that any statements written as fact have been
checked to the best of our abilities. However, we are still human, thankfully, and occasionally
little mistakes may crop up. Should this happen, please email info@nobrow.net with any erroneous
passages and we will be sure to amend the text accordingly for future editions of this book.

Professor Astro Cat's Human Body Odyssey © Flying Eye Books 2018.

This is a first edition published in 2018 by Flying Eye Books,
an imprint of Nobrow Ltd. 27 Westgate Street, London E8 3RL.

Text by Dr. Dominic Walliman and Ben Newman.
Illustrations by Ben Newman.

Dr. Dominic Walliman and Ben Newman have asserted their right under the Copyright,
Designs and Patents Act, 1988, to be identified as the Author and Illustrator of this Work.

Published in the US by Nobrow (US) Inc.

Printed in Poland on FSC® certified paper.

ISBN: 978-1-911171-91-1

FSC
MIX
Paper from
responsible sources
www.fsc.org FSC® C001693

Order from www.flyingeyebooks.com

PROFESSOR ASTRO CAT'S
HUMAN BODY
ODYSSEY

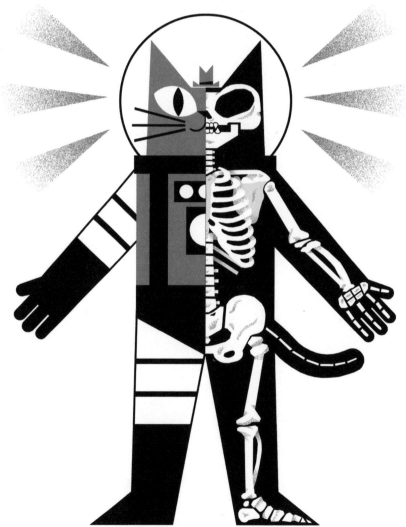

WRITTEN BY DR. DOMINIC WALLIMAN & BEN NEWMAN
ILLUSTRATED BY BEN NEWMAN

FLYING EYE BOOKS
LONDON – NEW YORK

Why is there so much hair on top of your head?
Hey, where is your funny bone? I want to make you laugh.
EVIE
DOMINIC
Are your ears supposed to be a weird shape?
Why are your eyes green?
GILBERT
What is the point of having skin?
Why do we sneeze? AAAAHHHHCHHHOOO!
MARTHA

Ah, greetings, science fans! You are just in time for our next adventure. We're going to be investigating something very, very important… **YOU!**

Yes, your human body is quite possibly one of the most complicated things in the Universe. All humans have a body, with similar shapes on the outside and pieces on the inside, but every single body is unique in its own wonderful way.

So get ready to join me, **Professor Astro Cat**, and my very knowledgeable friends as we embark on a **HUMAN BODY ODYSSEY!**

PARTICLE REDUCTION ORB
MULTI PERSON SHRINKING RAY

We've asked our good friend, Dr. Dominic Walliman, to be our guinea pig… uh, I mean test subject… no, uh… our human helper in this very special investigation into **human anatomy.**

FELICITY

ASTRO MOUSE

BEING ALIVE

If you are reading this, it means you are alive. Life can come in many shapes and sizes, and some life you can't see with your eyes alone. The science of studying all life, not just humans, is called **biology**. So what does it mean to be alive?

RESPIRATION

Most living things need food and air to survive. Oxygen in the air gives you energy to live.

SENSITIVITY

All life forms can sense and detect changes that happen around them. Humans do this with sight, sound, smell, touch and taste.

Haha, I can confirm that Martha is alive. She is sensitive to light!

MOVEMENT

Living things **react** to what happens around them. Humans move around to get food, and sometimes plants do too!

HII-YAA!

REPRODUCTION

Humans make more humans by having babies. This is called reproduction. If humans didn't reproduce, they would all eventually die out.

EXCRETION

Living things create chemicals that they need to get rid of to survive. This is why humans sweat, breathe out, and go to the bathroom.

NUTRITION

Life needs to take in and use food to grow and move.

GROWTH

Humans start as babies and grow into adults. All life grows in some way.

AT BIRTH 3 YEARS 6 YEARS   12 YEARS   25 YEARS

Sadly, old R.O.B.O. here might seem alive, but she needs to have all of the qualities of life to be truly living. For example, she can't grow or reproduce.

WHAT ARE YOU MADE OF?

Let's take a look at just how amazing your body is. The human body is made up of many different parts and **systems** that all work together in harmony automatically. It keeps you alive without you even needing to think about it. See for yourself!

Hair provides protection for the skin and helps keep you warm.

Eyes capture light so that you can see things.

Skin covers your whole body and protects everything inside you.

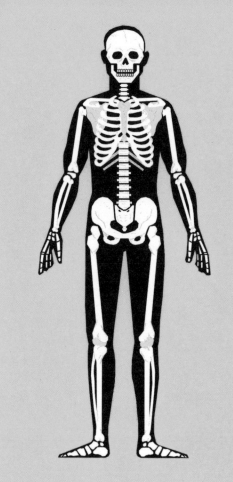

There are many **organs** inside your body that all have important jobs.

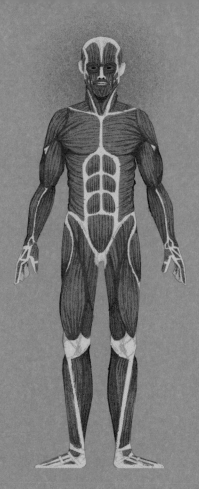

Bones make up the skeleton, which is the framework of your body.

Muscles pull on bones so that you can move.

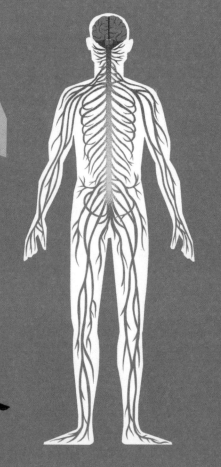

Nerves help send messages from your brain and spinal cord to the rest of your body.

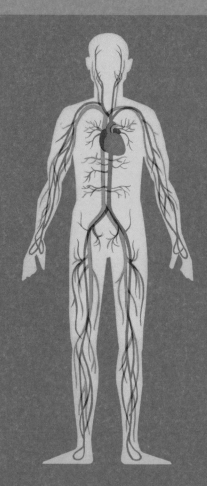

Arteries and **veins** take the blood pumped by the heart to different parts of the body.

VIEWING A MICROSCOPIC BODY

All of the different parts of the human body are made up of tiny living building blocks called **cells**, which are **microscopic**. This means that they cannot be seen by the human eye unless you use a **microscope** that magnifies very, very small things.

WHAT IS A CELL?

A **human cell** is a very small but fascinating structure. It has a protective skin called the **membrane**, a control center called the **nucleus**, and energy factories called the **mitochondria**. The inside of a cell is always a busy flurry of activity.

The **mitochondria** power the cell by breaking down sugars to produce energy.

The **cell membrane** acts like a wall that controls what goes in and out of the cell.

The **cytoplasm** is a gloopy jelly inside the cell where all its reactions happen.

Organelles sit in the cytoplasm and perform specific jobs, like organs do in the body.

A HUMAN CELL

The **nucleus** is like the brain of the cell and tells it what to do.

MICROSCOPE

7

YOUR CELLS

There are around 40 trillion cells in your body. 40 trillion is 40,000,000 million, which is more than you could ever imagine counting.

Not all cells are the same. There are around 200 different types in the human body, and they all have their own special jobs to do. Let's take a look at just a few of them!

RED BLOOD CELL

Red blood cells have a flat frisbee shape, and travel around your body delivering oxygen to all of your other cells. They are different from other cells because they don't have a nucleus.

RED BLOOD CELL

WHITE BLOOD CELL

EPITHELIAL CELL

WHITE BLOOD CELL

White blood cells are your body's soldiers, detecting and destroying any invading cells.

EPITHELIAL CELL

These cells squeeze together to make barriers inside and outside of your body, like your skin.

NERVE CELL

MUSCLE CELL

NERVE CELL

Our brains are made up of nerve cells that are wired all over the body to transmit electrical signals to and from the brain.

MUSCLE CELL

Muscle cells are long and flat, but can get shorter when they contract.

COMING TOGETHER

How do all these tiny cells make up a human?
Well, they need to stick together of course!

TISSUE

Many of the same cells can join together to make a **tissue**.
Muscle cells form muscle tissue and epithelial cells form epithelial tissue.

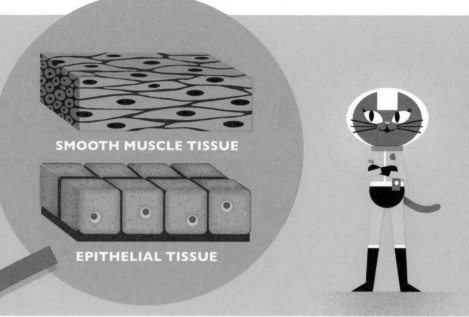

SMOOTH MUSCLE TISSUE

EPITHELIAL TISSUE

ORGANS

Several tissues join together to create an **organ**, such as the heart
or stomach. Organs perform very important jobs in the body.

STOMACH

Smooth
Muscle Tissue

Epithelial Tissue

SYSTEMS

Organs link together to create **organ systems**. There are 11 organ systems
in the human body, like the digestive system and the respiratory system.

**DIGESTIVE
SYSTEM**

ORGANISM

These organ systems work together to create an **organism,**
which in this case is the human body. Now isn't that just amazing?

HUMAN

Quick! I have a special invention that will help
us discover more about the human body.

THE SKELETON

All **206 bones** in your body connect together to form a framework called a **skeleton**. If you didn't have any bones, your skin and internal organs would be a messy, shapeless sack on the floor... and that would be terrible!

The **back bone**, or **spine**, keeps your body upright and is made up of 33 separate blocks of bone called **vertebrae**.

Oh no, the Professor has lost his bones!

I've built a pocket-sized X-ray projector so that we can have a good look at Dominic's **skeletal system**.

Your **cranium** (skull) protects your brain and sits on top of your neck vertebrae.

MANDIBLE
(lower jaw bone)

CLAVICLE
(collar bone)

HUMERUS

The **ribs** form a cage that protects vital organs, like the heart and lungs.

RADIUS

ULNA

PELVIS
(hip)

Each of your hands has 27 bones.

FEMUR
(thigh bone)

The bones in your body come in all shapes and sizes. The largest bone is the femur in your leg.

TIBIA
(shin bone)

DID YOU KNOW?

Your funny bone isn't actually a bone, it's a nerve in your elbow.

FIBULA

JOIN-T-ING IN!

The place where two bones meet, like your shoulder or elbow, is called a **joint**. Without joints, the human body would be as stiff as an ironing board. There are more than 300 joints in the human body and they allow different parts to move in various ways.

HINGE

Some joints, like elbows and knees, are **hinge joints** that can be bent or straightened.

Capsule covers the joint.

Synovial fluid helps the joint move.

Cartilage cushions the ends of the bones.

Ligaments hold the joint together.

BALL

Others, like our hips or shoulders, are **ball joints** that allow our legs and arms to point in many different directions.

BONE CUSHIONS

Our bones are very tough, so we have a firm but flexible material called **cartilage** in our joints that cushions them where they meet. A liquid called **synovial fluid** lubricates the joints and helps pieces of cartilage slip over one another.

One of the most useful joints in the human body is your **thumb** joint. It allows you to grip tools and do accurate work, like drawing a picture or making a machine.

Bones are five times stronger than steel, and even lighter because they are not completely solid. They have lots of tiny holes in them so they look a little like honeycomb in the middle.

Inside your bones is a thick, spongy jelly called **bone marrow** that helps make blood cells for your body.

BONE

MUSCLES

Although **joints** allow bones in the body to move, the movement is caused by the pull of sheets of tough tissue called **muscle**. Muscle tissue has the incredible ability to shorten (contract) itself so it can move the bone it is attached to. Without muscles, you would not be able move around.

PUMP IT!

There are over **640 skeletal muscles** that criss-cross and overlap all over the human body and give it its shape. The more you use a muscle, the stronger it gets. You have lots of different muscles that do many different things.

THE FASTEST MUSCLES AROUND

The fastest muscles in the human body are in the eye. They allow you to blink 5 times in one second.

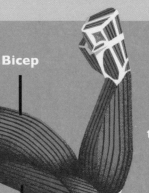

Bicep

Biceps and **triceps** move the arm.

Tricep

Abdominal muscles and **back muscles** let you bend forwards and backwards.

Forearm muscles move the hand and fingers.

Leg muscles let you stand upright and walk about.

The biggest muscle in the body is the **gluteus maximus** or… the buttock muscle!

THE POWER OF PULLING

Muscles can only pull and get shorter. Lots of muscles in our body work together and do opposite movements in order to move.

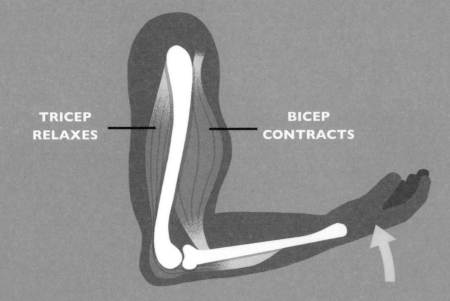

TRICEP RELAXES

BICEP CONTRACTS

When Dominic drops his forearm, his upper arm muscles are doing two things: the **tricep** is contracting, pulling the arm down, while the **bicep** is relaxing.

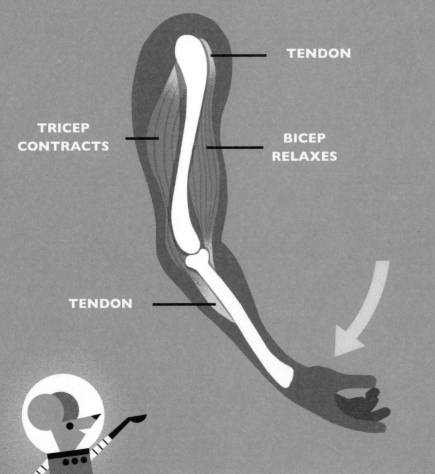

TENDON

TRICEP CONTRACTS

BICEP RELAXES

TENDON

THE TENDON CONNECTION

Skeletal muscles are connected to the bones with **tendons**, which are made of fibers of a very strong tissue called **collagen**.

OTHER IMPORTANT MUSCLES

Skeletal muscles are not the only type of muscle in the body. The two other types are the **cardiac muscles** and the **smooth muscles**.

The **cardiac muscle** works very hard all the time to keep your heart beating. Your heart can never take a break.

Smooth muscles are found around organs like your stomach. They work without you even thinking about it, like when they move food through your body.

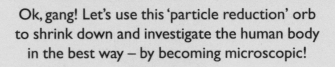

Ok, gang! Let's use this 'particle reduction' orb to shrink down and investigate the human body in the best way – by becoming microscopic!

Quick! While Dominic is eating his lunch, let's jump on him so we can explore the skin up close.

INCREDIBLE SKIN

It's amazing that the **skin** is actually an organ, and it's the biggest one you have! Your skin is like a suit of armour that holds all your muscles, bones and organs inside. It acts as a waterproof barrier that protects you and stops germs or viruses from getting in.

SENSITIVE FINGERS

Your fingertips are some of the most sensitive areas of your body because they are jam-packed with nerve endings. Fingernails help protect your sensitive fingers and grow out as hard extensions of the epidermis. They are made up of dead cells filled with **keratin**, which is a tough substance that your body also uses to create hair.

LEAVING YOUR MARK

The palms of your hand, the undersides of your fingers and the soles of your feet are covered in tiny ridges and grooves. These ridges help you to grip things, and the patterns they make are completely unique to you!

ON THE SURFACE

The surface of human skin is made up of thin layers of skin cells, sort of like a pad of notepaper. The dead cells on the top layer rub off during the day and are replaced by new skin cells from underneath. We call the outer layer of skin the **epidermis**, which is pronounced 'eh-pih-DUR-mis'.

RATHER FLAKY!

Your skin is constantly growing and falling off! You completely replace the outer layer of your skin about once a month, but where does it go? Well, you might see it floating in sunbeams or gathering on a shelf… we call it 'dust'!

Sweat glands are tiny holes that release sweat to cool the skin when it is hot.

Hair

Epidermis
close to the surface.

Nerves sense pressure, pain and temperature.

The **dermis** is the thicker layer underneath.

Hair muscle

The **hair follicle,** where hair grows.

Blood vessels bring blood full of nutrients and oxygen to feed the skin cells.

UNDER THE SKIN

Under the epidermis is a deep, thick layer called the **dermis,** which gives your skin its stretchiness. The dermis contains blood vessels to keep the skin supplied with food and oxygen, as well as sensors called nerve endings that help to detect changes in the body such as temperature, pressure and pain.

The **fat layer** stores energy and keeps us warm.

THE MOUTH

Humans use their mouths for grinding up food, drinking, breathing in air and speaking. Your teeth are even stronger than bones, and the muscles in your jaw mean you can chomp food into small pieces for the stomach to digest.

At the moment, Dominic's mouth is crunching up his lunch. You need to eat food to supply your body with important nutrients to keep it healthy.

TEETH

Did you know that you have 8 muscles in your tongue?

TONGUE

Whoooaaa! Why is it so slippery in here?

A TOOLBOX OF TEETH

An adult human has 32 teeth in their mouth. There are several different kinds of teeth that each have different uses.

Canines are like pincers and are used for piercing.

Incisors are like knives for cutting into food.

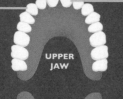

UPPER JAW

LOWER JAW

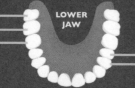

Molars are for grinding up food into little bits.

Premolars, between canines and molars, are for piercing and crushing.

SLIPPERY SPIT

When you chew food in your mouth, it gets mixed up with **saliva** that is a liquid squeezed out by your **salivary glands**. Saliva mixes with your food to make it softer and easier to swallow.

INSIDE THE TOOTH

A tooth has two main parts. The first is the crown, which sticks up out of the gum. The second is the root that is buried in the gum. Incisors and canines have only one root, while premolars and molars have two or three.

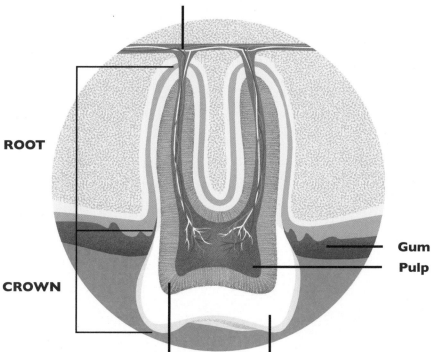

Nerve and **blood supply**

ROOT

CROWN

Gum

Pulp

Dentine is a yellow bone-like substance.

Enamel is the white outer layer of a tooth.

Hey, what are all these bumps on the tongue?

Those bumps on the tongue are called the **papillae.** The large papillae contain **taste buds** that are spread all over the tongue so you can taste whether something is sweet, salty, bitter, sour or savory.

KEEP THEM CLEAN!

Don't forget to brush your teeth in the morning and just before bed! Brushing twice a day will help keep your mouth healthy.

BRUSH YOUR TEETH
TWICE A DAY, EVERY DAY!

GOING DOWN

Both air and food go down the same tube at first: the **throat**. But if your food went into your lungs, it would make you choke, and if air got into your stomach, it would make you burp all the time. Fortunately, you have an **epiglottis** that flips down and blocks our windpipe (or **trachea**) when you swallow, directing food down your **esophagus** instead.

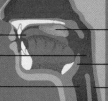

TONGUE
THROAT
TRACHEA
FOOD
EPIGLOTTIS
ESOPHAGUS

THE NOSE

Smell and taste are very closely linked because the nose and mouth are connected. This is why we've climbed up to explore the nose next! Most of your sense of taste is actually smell. You can test this yourself by holding your nose when you eat. Your food won't taste as good!

A UNIQUE STRUCTURE

The shape of your nose isn't formed by bone. It's mostly made of **cartilage**, which is softer. That is why it's a little bit squishy.

CARTILAGE

MUCUS

Snot helps you smell things! The thin layer of **mucus** inside your nose catches smell molecules and takes them to special smell receptors inside the nose. So if your nose was dry inside, you would have a hard time sensing smells.

Mucus traps dirt and germs before they get to your lungs. When you blow your nose, this mixture of snot, dust and germs is what comes out!

MUCUS

NASAL CAVITY

SMELL DETECTOR

That whiffy odor drifting up from Dominic's tuna sandwich comes with other particles, like germs and dirt, which are breathed up into his **nasal cavity.**

NOSTRIL

These **nasal hairs** in the **nostrils** stop flies or large bits of dust and pollen from going up your nose.

AIR GOES IN

OLFACTORY BULB

ODOR RECEPTOR CELL

Your nose produces nearly a quart of slimy snot every day!

THE ODOR DETECTIVE

Smells settle on a sticky and super-sensitive cell called an **olfactory receptor.** This receptor sends a signal to the brain through the **olfactory bulbs** and the smell is identified.

Your nose is so sensitive that it can tell the difference between 20,000 different smells!

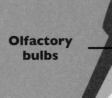

Olfactory bulbs

BLESS YOU!

If pollen, dust or other particles tickle or irritate your nose, it will clear itself when you **sneeze**. A sneeze can blast the irritable particles out at an incredible 100 miles an hour!

Don't forget to catch that sneeze in a tissue, otherwise the germs will fly everywhere.

THE EARS

Your ears allow you to hear your favorite music or a quiet whisper in class, but they also keep you aware of your surroundings. Even when you sleep, your ears are still on guard, filtering out sounds and listening for danger!

HOW DO WE HEAR SOUNDS?

Sounds are wobbles in the air that our ears collect and turn into signals for our brain. These wobbles have to travel through three main parts; the **outer ear**, the **middle ear** and the **inner ear**.

PINNA

TEMPORAL BONE

EAR CANAL

OUTER EAR

The air wobbles travel through the outer ear canal and hit the eardrum, making it vibrate.

EARLOBE

WAX ON, WAX OFF

The ear canal contains **wax** to stop specks of dirt from drifting too far into your ear. The tiny hairs in your ear help to brush the dirt back out. Both are very important for your ear because they help stop infections.

MIDDLE EAR

When the **eardrum** vibrates, it moves three very tiny, special bones called **ossicles,** back and forth rapidly. The ossicles are the smallest bones in the body. This vibration is then sent to the inner ear through the **oval window**.

HAMMER
(about the size of a grain of rice)

STIRRUP

ANVIL

INNER EAR

The inner ear is a maze of channels called the **cochlea** and the **semicircular canals**. These are filled with fluid, and the cochlea contains many hairs of different lengths that wobble with different sounds.

SEMICIRCULAR CANALS

AUDITORY NERVE SENDS INFORMATION TO THE BRAIN

OSSICLE

OVAL WINDOW

COCHLEA

EAR DRUM

BANG THAT DRUM

The **eardrum** is a thin, springy layer of tissue separating the air in the outer ear from the air in the middle ear.

A DELICATE BALANCE

Ears aren't just for hearing. They also help us **balance**. In the inner ear, the **semicircular canals** are three curved tubes that contain a fluid that sloshes around when you move, and stays still when you stop. Your brain checks the movement of the fluid to help you balance.

THE EYES

These delicate, golf-ball-sized spheres take in light to form pictures that help you make sense of the world. Everything around us is reflecting light and, like a camera, our eyes capture it. Our eyes need light to see, which is why it is difficult to see in the dark.

EYELID

RETINA

CHOROID

SCLERA

The **lens** and the **cornea** work together to focus light onto the retina.

Light rays come into our eye through the **cornea**, where they are then bent.

The **lens** changes shape automatically to focus on things that are different distances away.

CORNEA

PUPIL

The bent light rays go through a hole called the **pupil.**

IRIS

LENS

Behind the **lens** is a clear jelly-like fluid called the **vitreous humor**. This gives the eye its shape, otherwise it would look quite deflated.

Ciliary muscles

Ciliary muscles help the lens focus.

EYELASHES

ADJUSTING THE LIGHT

Eyes are so amazing that they adjust automatically to dim and bright lights, and can easily focus on things that are near or far away.

The **iris** controls the size of the **pupil** by relaxing or contracting itself to let more light in when it's dark, and less light in when it's bright.

DIM LIGHT

Iris
Pupil

BRIGHT LIGHT

Iris
Pupil

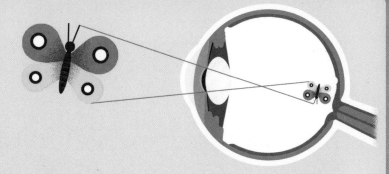

An upside-down image is formed on the **retina**, which is a blanket of two kinds of receptors: **rods** for seeing when there is very little light, and **cones** to detect colors and fine detail.

— RODS

— CONES

OPTIC NERVE

The **optic nerve** flashes signals from the retina to the brain and turns the upside-down image the right way up.

EYE MUSCLE

DEFENDING THE EYE

Your eyes sit within deep bowls in the skull called **eye sockets**. Eyes are very precious, so they need to be defended against everyday dirt and germs.

There are just six **eye muscles** that help each eye move in different directions and keep it attached to the eye sockets in the skull.

Eyebrows stop sweat from your forehead running into your eyes.

Eyelashes are great at stopping bits of dust or grit.

Tear ducts keep your eyes wet with salt water and flush out any dust or dirt that may land on your eye. Sometimes water leaks out of them when we are sad, in pain, or laughing too much!

Eyelids act as covers for the eyes. The muscles in the eyelid that help you blink are the fastest muscles in your whole body.

SEEING IN 3D

Try looking at a pencil up close with one eye, and then with the other. You'll notice that each eye sees the pencil at a different angle. Your brain puts both angles together to give you a sense of 3D perspective, and how far away something is.

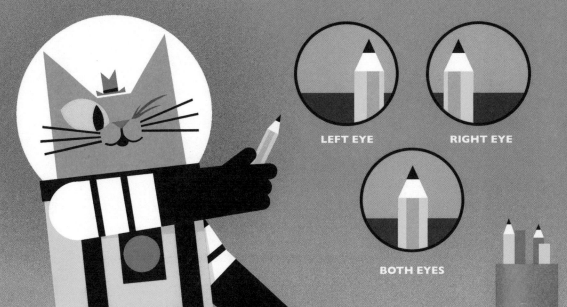

LEFT EYE

RIGHT EYE

BOTH EYES

THE BRAIN

As we travel along the optic nerve, we come to the **human brain**. Even though it's only about the size of a small cauliflower, the human brain is the most complicated structure that we know of. It is like a supercomputer that controls many vital parts of your body, like your five senses: **taste** (tongue), **smell** (nose), **hearing** (ears), **sight** (eyes) and **touch** (skin).

The pinky-grey and wrinkly outer layer of the brain is called the **cerebral cortex**.

This brain looks like an old walnut. It's so wrinkly!

The **cerebrum** controls your movement and coordination.

The **thalamus** is at the center of the brain and receives signals from the body.

The **hypothalamus** controls things that are automatic, like hunger, and keeps the body running smoothly.

The **olfactory bulbs** send signals about smell to the brain.

The **brain stem** connects the brain to the rest of the body. It is responsible for controlling basic functions like your breathing and heartbeat.

The **cerebellum** controls your balance, so when you walk or run somewhere, your arms and legs move together in harmony and you don't fall over.

A HEAD FULL OF NEURONS

The brain is made up of special nerve cells called **neurons**. Each of these cells has a **nucleus** like all the others, but it also has other very interesting parts.

WHAT A SHOCK!

Neurons fire signals to and from each other across the **synapse** from the **axon** to another's **dendrite**.

AXON is a very thin tail that sends messages to other neurons.

SYNAPSE is the connection between two neurons.

NUCLEUS

DENDRITES are these strange branches that receive messages from other neurons.

A GALAXY OF NEURONS

There are over a hundred billion neurons in the brain, which is about the same number as stars in our galaxy! If you were to lay out all the neurons from your brain in a line, they would stretch all the way from Earth to the moon....WHOA!

25

BRAIN FUNCTION

The brain is divided into two halves called **hemispheres**. It may seem strange, but the left side of your brain controls the right side of your body, and the right side of your brain controls the left side of your body. Each side of the brain is good at different things.

The **primary motor cortex** controls your muscles.

The **motor association cortex** coordinates difficult body movements.

The **primary somatosensory cortex** receives information from the skin.

The **prefrontal cortex** is where 'you' live. It is the place in the brain where your imagination, personality, and complex thoughts take place. This is where the brain learns.

The **sensory association area** makes sense of touch signals from the skin.

The **visual association area** makes sense of what you see.

Broca's area controls your speech.

The **visual cortex** detects what the eyes are seeing.

The **auditory cortex** detects sound from the ears.

Wernicke's area interprets language so you can communicate.

The **auditory association area** figures out the meaning of the sounds you hear.

MAPPING THE BRAIN

According to my map of the **left hemisphere**, different things happen in different areas of the brain.

All of these areas have to stay in touch with one another so you can do many things at the same time.

DID YOU KNOW?

Your brain uses about the same amount of power as a light bulb (20 watts).

THANKS FOR THE MEMORIES

You have two kinds of memory! **Short term memory** for remembering things that happened in the last 15-30 seconds, and **long term memory** to remember events that have happened to you throughout your life.

THINKING AND NOT THINKING

When you think about something, you are doing it consciously. We call this the **conscious mind**.

Sometimes you are not aware that your brain is busy thinking in the background. When the answer to a problem suddenly pops into your head, it is thanks to the **subconscious mind** for solving it for you.

NO TIME TO SLEEP

On average, you will spend over **25 years** of your life asleep, so it's fair to say that resting your body and brain is very important. Even though you might think your brain turns off when you go to sleep, it is in fact just as active as when you are awake. When you are asleep, your brain dreams!

DREAM LAND

When you are awake, your brain is too busy getting you safely through the day to process everything that happens around you, so it does this at night when you sleep. Nobody is exactly sure why you dream, but scientists think that it is because your brain is sifting through your recent experiences to store important **memories** and **learn**.

NIGHTMARES

Sometimes you have bad dreams that frighten you. This can happen when your brain is sorting through feelings like worry or stress. Your brain might even be thinking about something scary from a movie you saw recently! ARRRGGGHHHHH!

NERVOUS SYSTEM

Your brain receives messages and gives out orders, but it doesn't do this by phone or email. It uses electrical signals that travel through your **nervous system**, which is spread throughout your body. The nervous system is a **network** that helps control your split-second movements, your sensitivity to the world around you, and what is happening inside your body.

The nervous system's main highway from the brain is the **spinal cord**. A huge network of nerves branches off from the spinal cord to all the different limbs and organs in your body.

VERTEBRAE

CENTRUM is the body of the vertebrae

CARTILAGE
acts as a cushion between the vertebrae

THE COLUMN

The spinal cord is like the brain's tail. It runs almost all the way down your back through the **spinal column**, which protects it. This column is made up of 33 **vertebrae** that are shaped so that the spinal cord can run down the middle.

SPINAL CORD
protected by vertebrae

SPINAL NERVE

Our nervous system lets us sense the world around us and move our bodies in response to situations. This is especially important when we need to react fast!

Nerves send signals from our sensors, like our eyes and ears, to our brains through our nervous system.

When we move our body, electrical signals travel from our brain to our muscles.

Our nervous system allows us to move our bodies with great speed, accuracy and power.

Some reactions are fast reflex actions that stop us from getting hurt, like when you touch something hot and jump away from it. They are fast because the signals bypass the brain and go straight to the spinal cord.

With training, we can do amazing things with our nervous system!

THE LUNGS

Check this out! These two spongy windbags are your **lungs**, and they get oxygen into your body. Your body needs a constant supply of oxygen from the air, because your body's cells use it to burn sugar and fat to create energy.

VOCAL CORDS

RIGHT LUNG

TRACHEA

The **trachea** is where air comes into the lungs. It divides into two air pipes called the bronchi.

Rings of **cartilage** help keep the bronchi and trachea open.

BRONCHI

Each **bronchus** goes into a different lung. These pipes are lined with mucus and hairs to stop dust from getting into the lungs.

HEART

Your left lung needs to make room for your **heart**, so it is a little bit smaller than your right lung.

DIAPHRAGM

BRONCHIOLES

The **bronchioles** are tiny air pipes that branch off of the bronchi into smaller and smaller branches. Some are even narrower than a single hair!

30

LEFT LUNG

THE BRONCHIAL TREE

The bronchiole tubes that bring air into the lungs are known as the **bronchial tree** because they look like an upside-down tree.

ALVEOLI

Wow! Just look at these tiny air sacks at the ends of the bronchioles. They are called **alveoli**, and there are over 300 million of them in your body. The job of the **alveoli** is to move oxygen into your bloodstream using tiny tubes of blood called **capillaries**.

When oxygen is used up for energy, it travels through the blood and back to the lungs as a waste gas called **carbon dioxide**, which is released from the body when you breathe out.

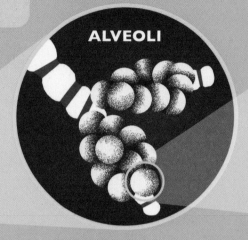

ALVEOLI

THE ART OF BREATHING

It's crazy to think that your lungs are full of tiny holes to make them light, and they don't even have any of their own muscles! Your lungs fill up with air, a bit like a sponge in water, and use the **intercostal muscles** from the rib cage and the **diaphragm** to help you breathe.

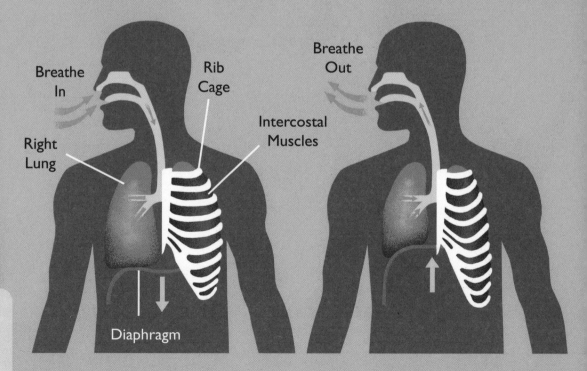

Breathe In

Right Lung

Rib Cage

Intercostal Muscles

Breathe Out

Diaphragm

BREATHING IN

When you breathe in, the intercostal muscles attached to the ribcage pull up and out while the diaphragm pulls down to drag air in, and your lungs swell up with air.

BREATHING OUT

When you breathe out, the intercostal muscles and diaphragm relax. The ribs close in and air is pushed out of our lungs through your mouth or nose.

HICCUPS

When your diaphragm becomes irritated from eating too quickly or breathing funny, it can make quick, jerky movements that bring air rushing through the throat. When the air suddenly hits your voice box (larynx), you make a strange 'hiccup' noise.

YOUR BLOOD

Look out! Things move pretty fast in the bloodstream. Your **blood** contains important nutrients and oxygen that it transports to all your cells at breakneck speed. Then, it collects all of the waste material and quickly takes it to the right place for your body to get rid of it.

WHAT IS BLOOD?

Just over half of your blood is made of a watery liquid called **plasma**. The rest of your blood is made up of three types of cells: **red blood cells, white blood cells**, and **platelets**.

Your **red blood cells** are amazing! They carry oxygen around your body and help transport carbon dioxide away so that your body can get rid of it. It is the red blood cells that give your blood its red color.

White blood cells are bigger than red blood cells, and help guard your body from attack. They are like the body's police force, swimming around looking for bad cells and then fighting them off.

Platelets are special cells that help to heal wounds and tears in your tissue. If you have an accident and cut your skin, it is the **platelets** that stick together to stop the bleeding so that other cells can repair the skin.

A SINGLE DROP

In a single drop of blood, there are about 150 million red blood cells, 250,000 white blood cells and 10 million platelets.

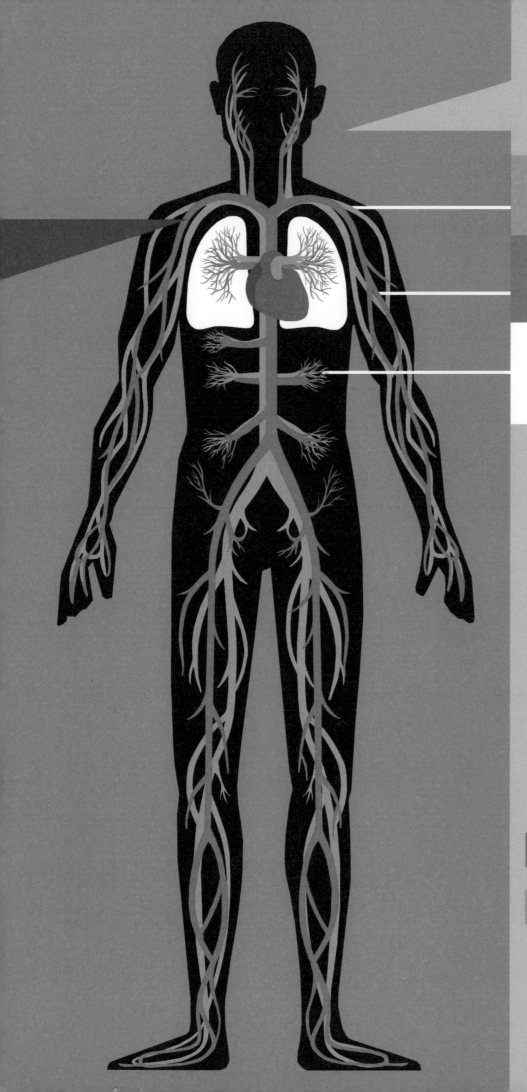

THE BLOOD SYSTEM

The blood system is spread throughout the whole body by a network of different blood vessels called **arteries**, **capillaries** and **veins**.

Veins are thinner than arteries and carry blood from our organs and tissues back to our heart.

Arteries carry blood away from the heart.

Capillaries are the smallest parts of the network. They carry the blood through our organs and tissues. In the capillaries, blood gives up oxygen to the cells in our body and absorbs carbon dioxide.

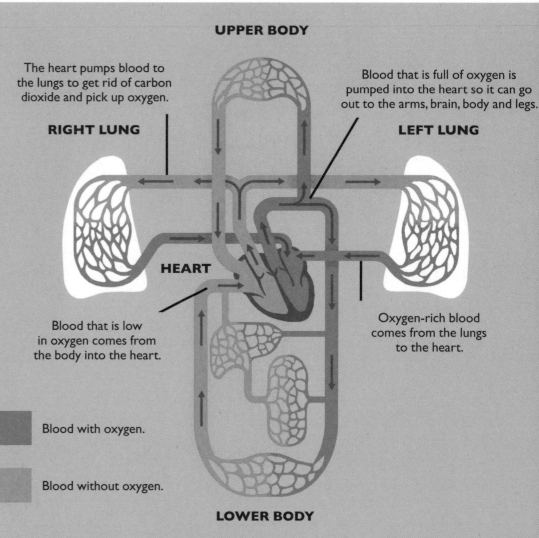

UPPER BODY

The heart pumps blood to the lungs to get rid of carbon dioxide and pick up oxygen.

Blood that is full of oxygen is pumped into the heart so it can go out to the arms, brain, body and legs.

RIGHT LUNG

LEFT LUNG

HEART

Blood that is low in oxygen comes from the body into the heart.

Oxygen-rich blood comes from the lungs to the heart.

Blood with oxygen.

Blood without oxygen.

LOWER BODY

AROUND THE WORLD

We have so many blood vessels in our body that if we laid them out end to end, they would stretch around the world two and a half times!

YOUR HEART

Easily the hardest working muscle in your body is the **heart**! It may only be about the size of your fist, but your heart has the tireless job of continuously pumping blood around your body all day and all night for your whole life.

In just one day, an adult's heart beats about one hundred thousand (100,000) times. A child's heart is a little faster, beating at around one hundred and fifty thousand (150,000) times a day.

↑ **Red arrows mean blood with oxygen in it.**

↑ **Blue arrows mean blood that has lost its oxygen.**

A COMPLICATED ARRANGEMENT

The heart is a complicated arrangement of **pipes** and **chambers** that are designed to pull blood in and pump it out. The heart uses **valves** to operate a strict one-way system for your blood to follow.

On the right side, low-oxygen blood is pumped to the lungs and on the left side, high-oxygen blood is pumped to the body. With each beat, the heart performs two steps. Lub-dub. Lub-dub.

Blood that is full of oxygen is pumped around the body.

Blood that is pumped to the lungs to collect oxygen.

Blood from the lungs that is full of oxygen.

Left atrium

Right atrium

Valve

Valve

Valve

Left ventricle

Right ventricle

Blood from the body that has lost its oxygen.

EXPRESS DELIVERY

In just 45 seconds, the heart can pump blood around your entire body.

LUB

Blood starts off in the two entrances to the heart called the **right atrium** and **left atrium**. These atria contract and push the blood into the main chambers called the **right ventricle** and the **left ventricle**. Then, a valve closes on each side to stop blood from flowing backwards.

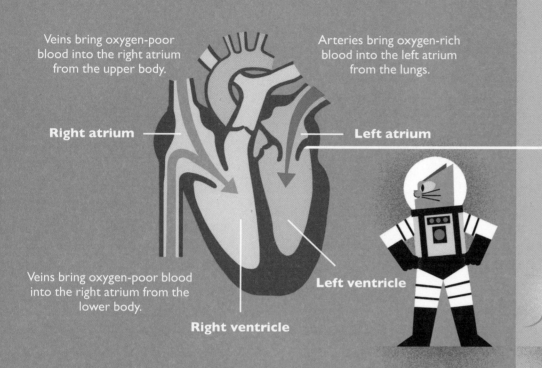

Veins bring oxygen-poor blood into the right atrium from the upper body.

Arteries bring oxygen-rich blood into the left atrium from the lungs.

Right atrium

Left atrium

Veins bring oxygen-poor blood into the right atrium from the lower body.

Left ventricle

Right ventricle

DUB

The two ventricles contract, pushing blood out of the heart. Again, a valve closes on each side to stop blood from flowing backwards.

The **cardiac muscles** in the heart are special because they can keep on working without ever getting tired. They are constantly pumping to keep the blood going around your body.

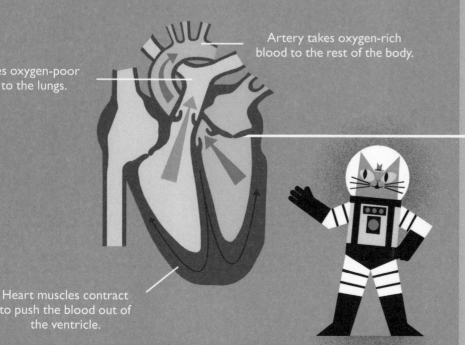

Vein takes oxygen-poor blood to the lungs.

Artery takes oxygen-rich blood to the rest of the body.

Heart muscles contract to push the blood out of the ventricle.

VALVES

Valves are amazing structures that let blood flow one way, but stop it from flowing in the opposite direction. They make sure that our blood only goes one way through our heart and keeps circulating around our body.

OPEN VALVE

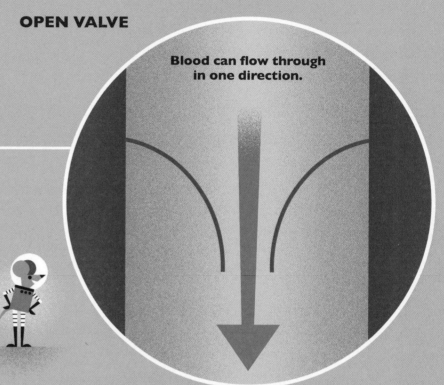

Blood can flow through in one direction.

Even though they are as thin as tissue paper, valves are very strong and will open and close 6 billion times in an average lifetime!

CLOSED VALVE

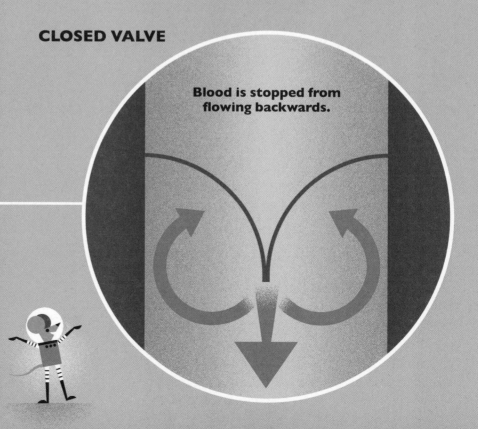

Blood is stopped from flowing backwards.

DIGESTION

Human bodies can't run on air alone; they need fuel to keep going! Your body needs the energy from the different chemicals and nutrients in food and water to keep working and repair itself. The breaking-down and absorption of food in the body is called **digestion**.

SALIVARY GLANDS

MOUTH

Food is chewed by your teeth and broken down by the spit in your mouth. Your spit, or **saliva**, contains special proteins called **enzymes** that help soften food so it can slide down your throat and into your stomach.

THROAT

Food passes through the **esophagus**

Once you've finished chewing and swallowing your food, it takes a group of organs working together as a team to digest it. Get ready, gang! It looks like things are about to get a bit sticky as we venture into the **digestive system**!

ENZYMES

Enzymes are special proteins that the body produces to help break down your food. There are many different kinds of enzyme produced by the **mouth**, **stomach**, **liver** and **pancreas**.

LIVER

GALL BLADDER

STOMACH

PANCREAS

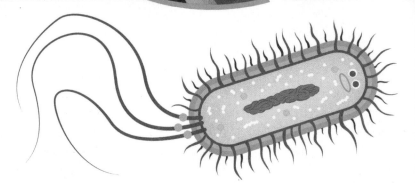

BACTERIA

Bacteria are single-celled microorganisms called **microbes** or **germs**. There are billions of different bacteria in your digestive system that help process your food and release useful nutrients. Some bacteria are 'friendly' and help your body, while other bacteria can cause infections and can make you sick.

The **gall bladder** releases bile into your digestive system, where it is used to break down large droplets of fat into smaller droplets so that they are easier to digest.

STOMACH

In the stomach, food is squeezed and mashed up with **gastric juices**. These juices contain **enzymes** that break the food down further and kill any germs that might try to make you sick.

The food is slowly released over four hours, but I think we should get out of here right now!

LARGE INTESTINE

Once the food is fully digested, it passes into the large intestine as a watery waste material. The water from the watery waste is sucked out and put back into the body through the bloodstream. The bits that the body doesn't want any more are turned into **feces**.

SMALL INTESTINE

It is the small intestine's job to absorb the nutrients from your liquidized food. These nutrients pass through the intestine's lining and into your bloodstream.

The walls of the small intestine are covered with tiny finger-like things called **villi** that help absorb and break down your food.

RECTUM

The solid, unwanted waste is passed out of the body as **feces**, or poop, through the **rectum** and then released by the **anus**. Uh… I think we'll go back the other way, guys!

THE TIME TO PASS

It takes about 36 hours for food to go through your whole digestive system.

YOUR LIVER

Your liver is the biggest internal organ in your body. It is very good at multi-tasking, since it does over **500 different jobs**. Your liver is always a hive of activity and plays an important role in your digestion by sorting out which things your body needs and which things it doesn't!

TOXIC TOXINS

The liver turns good stuff into things that your body can use and removes bad things it doesn't need, like poisonous **toxins**. Toxins come from food or are produced by your body to help break down the food.

HOW THE LIVER WORKS

Gosh, it's so busy in here! Although your liver does many different things, they can be broken down into three simple processes; **cleansing, production** and **storage**.

REGENERATION

The liver is specially equipped to deal with poisons, and it is the only organ that can grow back to its original size even if only a quarter of it is left. It can do this really fast and still work as usual while the regeneration happens. Amazing!

CLEANSING

Your liver cleans toxins from your blood, making them harmless, and then lets bile wash them away through the digestive system. This is one of your liver's most important jobs!

PRODUCTION

When digesting, your body uses fat from your food. Your liver produces a thick, yellowy-green digestive juice called **bile** that helps absorb fat, or **cholesterol**, into your bloodstream. Bile is stored in your **gall bladder** until it is ready to use.

STORAGE

Your body needs **carbohydrates**, which are a form of energy found in foods like bread and milk. Carbohydrates are broken down by the digestive system into a type of sugar called **glucose**.

YOUR BODY'S PANTRY

Your body keeps supplies of the different nutrients it needs. When you eat food, the important chemicals are extracted and some are stored in the liver to be used later.

GLYCOGEN

Your cells burn glucose as fuel to do things. Glucose is stored as glycogen in your liver and muscles, ready for when you need a power boost.

VITAMINS are organic substances that come from plants or animals. They do lots of different things in your body to keep you healthy and repair damage.

MINERALS are simple elements that come from the earth. Calcium is good for your bones, and iron helps your red blood cells to carry oxygen around your body.

KIDNEYS

Next, we're over to the **kidneys**! You have one on either side of your spine. Your kidneys are another type of organ that cleans and removes poisonous waste from the body after all the good stuff has been absorbed.

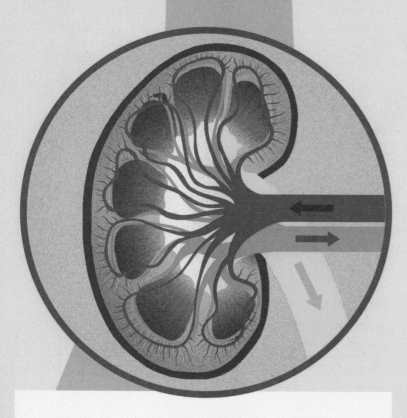

WHY TWO?

Although you have two kidneys, you can survive just fine with only one. So why do we have an extra kidney rather than a spare heart or liver?

Scientists think that when you are growing inside your mother, you grow the same on each side. If you draw a line from your nose down through your belly button, you'll see that one side is like a mirror image of the other.

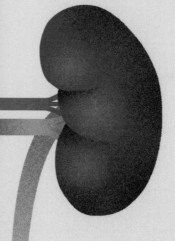

— **URETER**

EXPELLED!

Just like your intestines expel waste from food and your lungs expel carbon dioxide gas, your kidneys filter your blood to remove waste or poisonous toxins. These toxins are combined with salt and water to make **urine**, or pee, which is then expelled from the body.

After the blood has been through the kidneys and is all clean, it goes back into the blood system to carry on its job.

BLADDER —

URETHRA —

THE CLEANEST BLOOD AROUND

Your kidneys will filter your blood up to 400 times a day!

BLADDER

Once the kidneys have washed out all the toxins, salt and water, the urine is sent down a tube called the **ureter** to the **bladder**. The bladder is like a stretchy bag that stores your urine until you need to pee.

WATER BALLOON

Think of the bladder like a water balloon. It is small, but can get much bigger when it's filled with liquid. At some point, you'll need to empty your bladder, so nerves in the wall of your bladder will send a signal to your brain that tells you to go pee. Quick, to the bathroom!

HOLD TIGHT

The urine is held in by a special ring-shaped muscle called a **sphincter** that squeezes the exit tube closed. When we pee, the sphincter muscle relaxes while the bladder walls squeeze together. This pushes the urine out through the **urethra** and into the toilet.

WHAT'S IN YOUR URINE?

You might notice that your pee is yellow in the morning, but as you drink more water throughout the day, it gets lighter. This is because there is less waste in your urine at the end of the day than there is in the morning. In fact, around 95% of your urine is water.

LYMPHATIC SYSTEM

Another set of tubes that runs through the whole body… this must be the **lymphatic system**! The lymphatic system works alongside the blood system to keep the insides of your body clean and free of germs. The lymphatic system contains several organs: the **spleen**, **tonsils**, **thalamus gland** and **adenoids**.

LYMPH NODES

HEART

SPLEEN

LYMPH FLUID

This system of tubes is grouped together in clusters called **nodes** and carries a fluid just as important as blood: **lymph**. Lymph fluid is made up of about 97% plasma. Remember, plasma is the clear part of your blood!

The largest lymphatic organ is the **spleen**. It contains lymphocytes and catches and recycles red blood cells when they are old or damaged.

ISN'T THAT JUST SWELL?

You might notice that your lymph nodes swell up when you are ill. Your lymph nodes are microscopic battlegrounds where invading germs are fought off by special white blood cells called **lymphocytes**. This keeps infections away and lets your body heal.

ENDOCRINE SYSTEM

The nervous system isn't the only way of sending a message around your body. There is another system, called the **endocrine system**. While the nervous system uses electrical pulses to transmit messages, the endocrine system uses special chemicals called **hormones** that move through the bloodstream.

HORMONES

Hormones control many processes inside your body. They affect your mood and your growth by letting other cells know what to do. Hormones are released by **glands**, and there are many different glands in your body.

The **pineal gland** is in the middle of the brain. It creates a hormone called **melatonin** that helps make you sleepy at night and wakes you up in the morning.

The **thyroid gland** releases two hormones that control how fast the cells in your body turn food into energy.

The **adrenal glands** sit at the top of each kidney. One hormone they release is **adrenaline**, which makes your heart pound faster when you get a fright. This is very useful if you suddenly need to run away from danger!

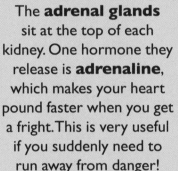

The **pituitary gland** sits at the bottom of your brain. Even though it is only the size of a pea, it is very important because it controls all the other glands by sending out chemical messages.

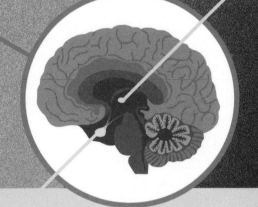

The **pancreas** releases two hormones that control the amount of sugar in your blood: **insulin** and **glucagon**. These are important because you need a steady supply of sugar in your blood to give your cells energy. You don't want too much of it or too little.

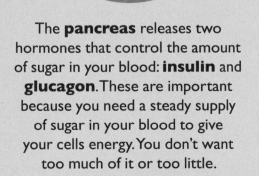

IMMUNE SYSTEM

There are many germs and viruses out in the world. Your body's defense against these germs is called the **immune system**, and it fights to stop you from getting sick.

THE INVADERS

"**Germ**" is a general name for a bad cell that will cause havoc inside your body. There are three main kinds of germ: **bacteria**, **viruses** and **fungi**.

Bacteria are small, single cells that exist everywhere on Earth. They have no nucleus, unlike human cells, and some have a tail-like part to help them spin and move around.

Most bacteria are friendly and help you, like the ones in your digestive system that help to digest your food. However, some forms of bacteria are harmful and can cause **bacterial infections**, like food poisoning or pneumonia.

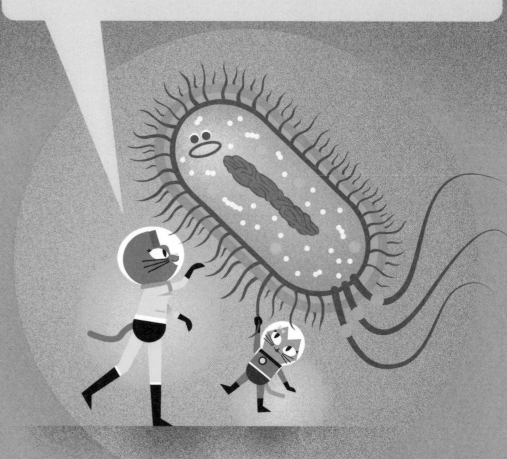

Viruses are tiny microorganisms, even smaller than bacteria, that cannot reproduce on their own. The only way they can reproduce is by invading a living cell, taking it over, and making it produce of a copy of itself.

The flu and chicken pox are both caused by viruses. It can be difficult to stop viruses because they change, or mutate, very quickly.

Fungi are made of cells with a nucleus, and can cause fungal infections like athlete's foot.

THE BODY DEFENDERS

The first defense against germs is to stop them from getting into your body in the first place.

Your **skin** acts like a barrier to stop bacteria from getting in, and the sweat on the surface of your skin kills bacteria.

The **mucus** in your nose traps bacteria. They get stuck, like your feet when walking through mud.

Your **saliva** has an antibacterial enzyme in it to kill germs that come in through your mouth.

Your **stomach** has strong acid in it that kills germs in our food.

AN ARMY OF CELLS

Oops, I think Dominic has cut his hand! Don't worry, his **white blood cells** are ready for action to stop any infection. Release the second line of defense!

Look! Here come the **B lymphocytes**. They create special substances called **antibodies** that stick to the invading germs so the body can track them.

Now it's time for the soldiers to take control. The **T cell** finds the invaders with the help of the antibodies, and starts to attack them. The T cells can call in extra help from big cells like **phagocytes**, who eat and destroy the germs using powerful enzymes.

If you see a yellow liquid called **pus** in your cut, it is made up of white blood cells, called **monocytes**, as well as dead bacteria from the battle to heal an infection.

REPRODUCTION

If humans didn't make more of themselves, they would not exist. Humans make copies of themselves by **reproducing**. Two different individuals need to mate to create a new organism. In humans, you need female and male reproductive cells to make a baby.

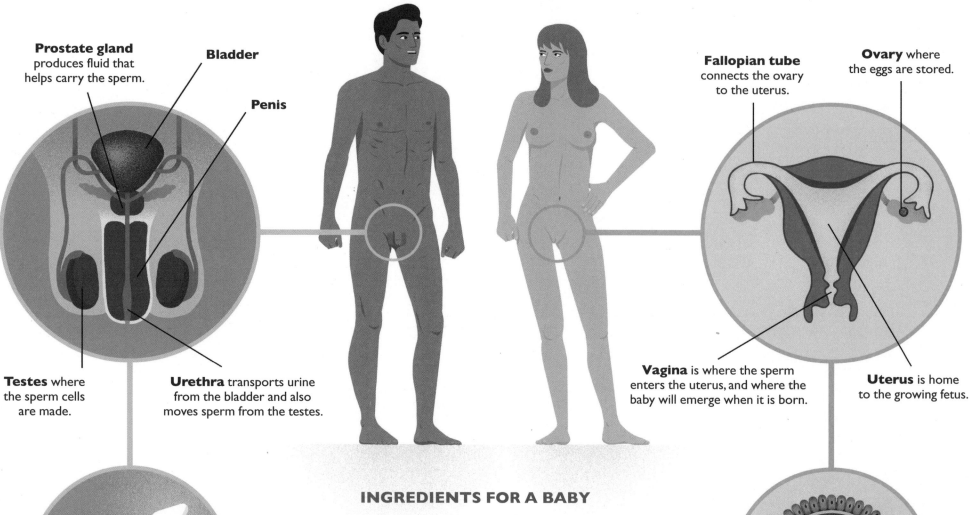

Prostate gland produces fluid that helps carry the sperm.

Bladder

Penis

Testes where the sperm cells are made.

Urethra transports urine from the bladder and also moves sperm from the testes.

Fallopian tube connects the ovary to the uterus.

Ovary where the eggs are stored.

Vagina is where the sperm enters the uterus, and where the baby will emerge when it is born.

Uterus is home to the growing fetus.

INGREDIENTS FOR A BABY

To make a baby, you need two ingredients. One part is **sperm cells** that are formed in the man's testes. The sperm cells are carried through tubes and released through the **penis**.

The other part is the **egg cells** that form in the woman's **ovaries**. One egg is released every month. Women release about 300 to 400 egg cells during their reproductive lives.

SPERM

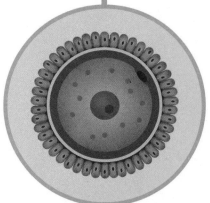

EGG

A PRODUCTIVE MEETING

The egg cell only allows one sperm cell inside. The nucleus of the sperm cell contains half of the information to make a human, and the nucleus of the egg cell contains the other half. They fuse together to fertilize the egg cell with all the information it needs to make a new human.

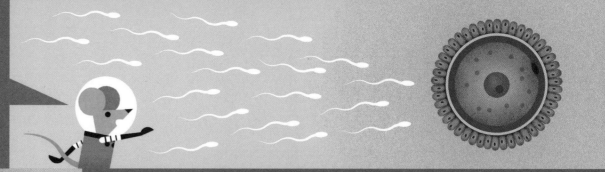

RACE TO THE EGG

A baby is made when a **sperm cell** meets an **egg cell** inside a woman's **fallopian tube**, joining together to form a **fertilized egg**. Sperm cells have wriggling tails that move them forward to try and find the egg.

GROWING LIFE

In the woman's womb, the cell divides over and over again and starts to turn into specialized cells, like skin cells, brain cells, and other cells that form organs. They all combine to create a **fetus**.

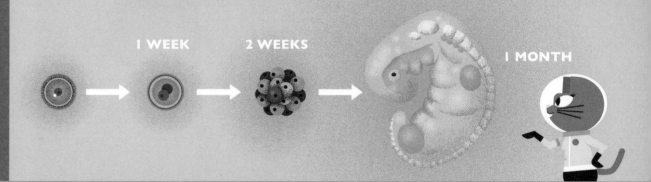

I WEEK   2 WEEKS   I MONTH

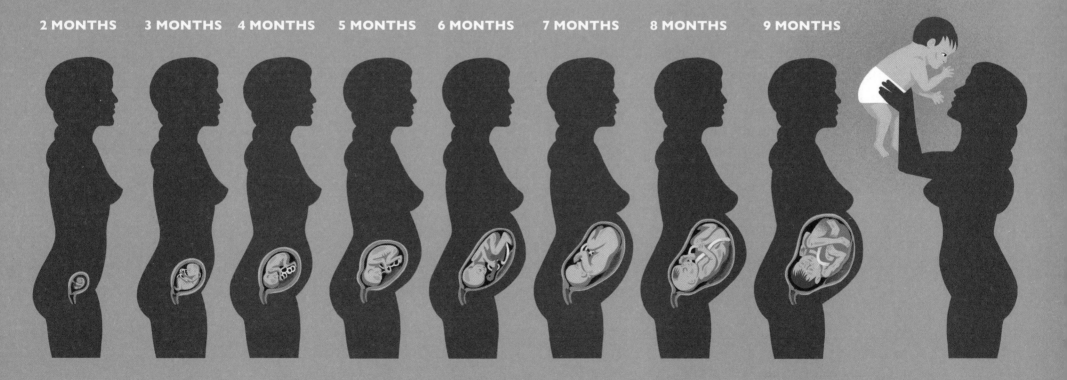

2 MONTHS   3 MONTHS   4 MONTHS   5 MONTHS   6 MONTHS   7 MONTHS   8 MONTHS   9 MONTHS

CARRYING LIFE

When a woman has a fetus developing inside her, she is **pregnant**. She shares her oxygen and the nutrients in her blood with the growing fetus through a special organ called the **placenta**. The fetus is connected to the placenta with the umbilical cord.

You can see where your **umbilical cord** was attached to you because it is where your belly button is now.

The fetus grows bigger and bigger, and after 9 months the baby is ready to be born.

GROWING UP

I think it's time we returned to our normal size to help explain this bit about humans. Over time, babies grow into children, then into teenagers and eventually adults. The growth and changes that take place in your body are called **aging**.

THE WONDER YEARS

In your teenage years, your body goes through some big changes called **puberty**. This happens earlier for girls, at around 10 to 12 years old, and later for boys, at about 12 to 14.

THE EARLY YEARS

Babies grow into infants very quickly after they are born. They start to make sense of the world as they learn to crawl, walk and talk.

When you are a child, your body grows taller and your brain develops really fast as you learn lots of new things. Books are a great way to help your brain!

Puberty has effects on the body like growth spurts and the development of your reproductive system. You also start to grow hair in places other than the top of your head! This is all controlled by **hormones**, and a side effect of these hormones is that you might get some red spots, or zits, on your skin.

WHERE DO WRINKLES COME FROM?

There are fibers in your dermis called elastin that keep your skin stretchy. As you grow older, your dermis loses its elastin and becomes thinner, so you get wrinkles. Don't worry, parents! Wrinkles just mean that you are wise and experienced.

AGING GRACEFULLY

If you exercise and eat healthy food throughout your life, you can stay healthy long into old age, even as your body slows down. Looking after your body when you are young will really help when you get older – just ask your parents!

ALL GROWN UP

When you reach adulthood, your body keeps changing, but it happens much, much slower. Between 20 and 30 years old, your reproductive system is at its peak, which means that this is the easiest time to make babies.

As you grow older, your hair can lose its color and turn grey or silver. This normally starts happening in your 30s.

GENETICS

My uncle Alfonso and I are from the same family. Although he is older than me, you can see a family resemblance. People may have told you that you look like a member of your family, like your mother or father. This is because you might share the same **genes**.

Hey! Check out my new jeans!

IT'S ALL IN THE GENES

Ha, not your denim jeans, Gilbert! We're talking about the genes you got from your biological parents. You got half of your genes from your mother's egg and half from your father's sperm. You might have your father's eyes and your mother's hair, or the other way around!

FATHER + **MOTHER** = **FELICITY**

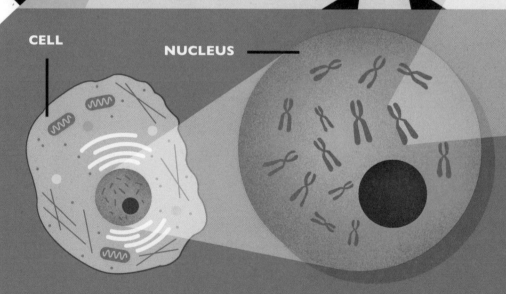

CELL

NUCLEUS

GENE GENIE

Every single cell in your body contains around **30,000 genes** that carry the information, or code, that makes you, **you**! Your genes are stored in spaghetti-like things called **chromosomes**, which are coiled up into an 'X' shape inside the nucleus of your cells.

YOUR BODY'S INSTRUCTION MANUAL

Human cells contain a nucleus with 46 chromosomes in, and each chromosome is made up of **deoxyribonucleic acid**, or, more easily put, **DNA**. Imagine a long piece of tape where all the instructions about how to make you have been written out. That is a bit like your DNA.

FEMALE OR MALE?

When you are born, a doctor assigns your sex based on what chromosomes you have. These are called **sex chromosomes**, and are arranged in two different pairs depending on your biological sex. **Females** have two 'X' chromosomes, while **males** have an 'X' chromosome and a 'Y' chromosome.

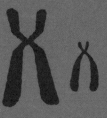

(XX) FEMALE

(XY) MALE

CHROMOSOME

A STRETCH BEYOND

DNA is super, super small and wrapped up incredibly tightly. If you unraveled all the DNA from one of your cells, it would be six and a half feet long. If you took all the DNA from your entire body and put it end to end, it would reach to the sun and back 600 times!

DNA is tightly wound so…

…it needs to be unwound a lot for you to find the double helix.

BASES

DNA Double Helix

THE DNA SPIRAL

Your DNA looks like a ladder that has been twisted end to end into a shape called a **double helix**. The sides of the ladder are made of sugar and phosphates, and the rungs are made of special chemicals called **bases**.

KEEPING HEALTHY

Has anyone ever told you, "you are what you eat"? Well, this is actually very true, because all of the cells in your body are made from the molecules of the food that you digest. Think about how crazy that is! You are like a mixture of pizzas, salad, bananas and sandwiches!

NUTRITION

Eating well is really important to stay healthy and grow tall and strong. Knowing which foods are good for your body is called **nutrition**. The basics of nutrition are simple: have a varied diet with lots of fresh fruits and vegetables, and avoid too much processed food. So what exactly is in food?

PROTEIN

You need **protein** to repair your body, stay healthy and grow tall. Lots of natural food has protein, but you get the most protein from meat, cheese and nuts.

CARBOHYDRATES

All of the cells in your body need energy to do their jobs and to multiply. This energy comes from a sugar called **glucose**, which comes from **carbohydrates** in your food like bread, pasta, rice and vegetables.

VITAMINS AND MINERALS

Dairy foods, like milk and cheese, are high in **calcium**, which is a **mineral** you need for strong bones and teeth. They are also high in **vitamin B12**, which your nerves need to work properly.

FAT

Fat is essential for storing and retrieving energy and to transport vitamins around your body. You can find fat in foods like olives, nuts and meat.

TOO MUCH PROCESS

All food starts with raw ingredients: plants or animals that have come from a farm. Processing turns the raw ingredients into food. If it is processed too much, some of the nutritional parts are lost, and harmful chemicals can build up. That is why it is always best to make food out of raw ingredients.

YOUR CHOICE

Food is so varied and important to life that people make decisions about food based on their beliefs. Some people don't eat meat and are called **vegetarians**, and some people called **vegans** don't eat anything that comes from animals (like meat, eggs, and milk).

LOVE FOOD, LOVE LIFE

The most important thing to remember is to enjoy good food. There are few things in life as satisfying as eating a good, nutritious meal. It always puts a smile on my face!

MEDICINE

Sometimes you get sick or have an accident, and your body can't fix the problem on its own. Fortunately, there are lots of other humans out there who can help you get better.

When you are sick, you go to see a **doctor** who will figure out what's wrong and how to make you better. They can figure out what the best treatment is by asking you questions and doing tests.

BAD BACTERIA

Sometimes, even though your body is trying to fight them off, small bacteria can cause an **infection** and make you feel very sick. Doctors can give you an **antibiotic**, which is a medicine made by humans to kill harmful bacteria.

VIRAL INFECTIONS

Viruses are different from bacteria, so antibiotics don't work against them. Your body can build amazing defenses against a virus to stop it from attacking again. This is called **immunity**, and means that you will not get sick from that particular virus in the future. You normally only ever get chickenpox once, because your body becomes immune to it.

AAACHOOOO!

Sadly, you will get many colds in your life because the cold virus keeps changing. So each time you get a cold, your body needs to figure out a new way of beating it.

CREATING A CURE

Doctors can keep you from getting sick with **vaccines**. A vaccine is an injection that teaches your body how to fight a disease. Before vaccines, lots of people would become very sick and die from diseases like measles or polio. Vaccines have helped make humans immune to these illnesses.

BROKEN BONES

If you break a bone, you need to go to a hospital and have an X-ray scan. This lets the doctors see where the broken bone is inside your body. Then, they can re-set the bone in the right place and put it in a cast to stop it from moving around. Eventually, your bone will naturally heal by itself.

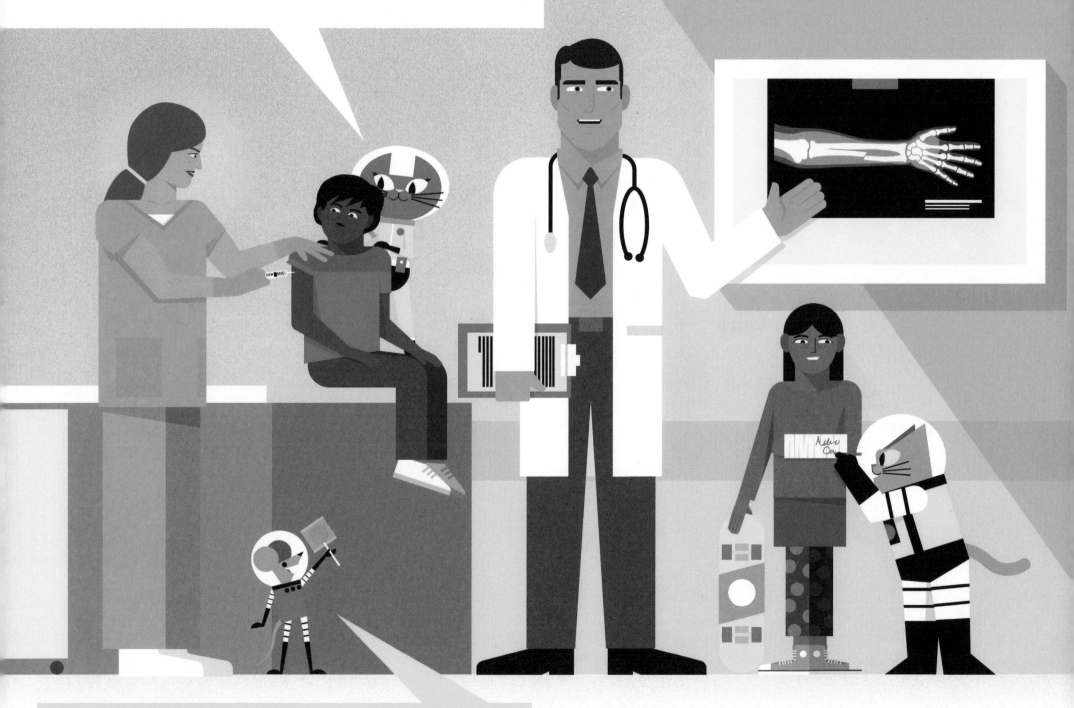

The more people who are immunized against a disease, the harder it is for the disease to spread and hurt other people. Getting immunized helps you and everyone you meet.

EXERCISE

The best and most fun way to stay healthy is through exercise. Not only does it boost your immune system, it also makes you stronger and faster. This helps burn off fat, protect you from injuries and lower your blood pressure, which is good for the heart.

DISABILITIES

Some people are born with bodies that are different, and some people might lose parts of their bodies during their life from accidents or illnesses. This is known as a **disability**. The human body and mind are incredibly adaptable, so regardless of a disability you can still live a comfortable life.

Disabilities come in many different forms: some affect your body, and some are not always immediately visible as they affect your brain.

PROSTHETIC LIMBS

Arms and legs are called limbs. If you are without an arm or a leg, you might use a **prosthetic limb**. Prosthetic means artificial, as these limbs are made by humans to fit your body.

Right now, humans are building more advanced prosthetic limbs, like **robotic limbs** that move by receiving commands from your muscles, just like real arms and legs.

STAYING MOBILE

If you find it difficult to walk, you can use a mobility device to get around. You will most likely use a **wheelchair** to sit in and push the wheels with your hands to get around. There are also wheelchairs with electric motors if you have difficulties using your hands.

READING WITH FEELING

If you are blind or have limited vision, you won't be able to use your eyes to read words. Instead, you can read **braille** with your fingers. Each letter is made up of a different pattern of bumps that you touch to read.

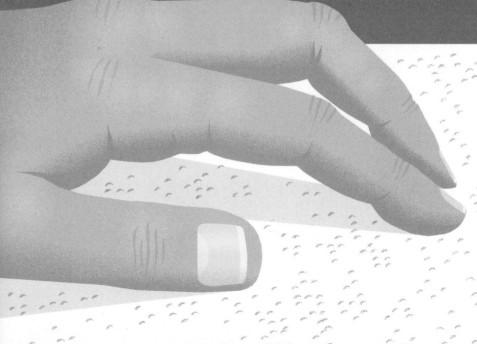

PARDON?

If you cannot hear very well, you can get a hearing aid that makes sounds louder. If your inner ear doesn't work properly, you can get a cochlear implant, which sends sound signals directly to the brain along the auditory nerve.

JUMBLED

If you have **dyslexia**, you have difficulties recognizing speech sounds and how to connect them with things you read. This can make it very hard to read and remember how to spell. Dyslexia takes time to overcome because you need to learn how your brain works and find alternative ways of learning words and letters.

Depression takes place in your brain and can be very upsetting for the person suffering from it. Imagine if you could not control your emotions: you might feel unbelievably sad and not know why. Even small, everyday things can trigger huge emotions.

INVISIBLE PROBLEMS

Some disabilities are in the brain. Although you might not be able to see them, they are still very much there.

HUMANS CAN HELP

To overcome this, it is best to talk to a doctor or a therapist who is trained to help. Sometimes you can be helped with special medicines, or you can learn over time to cope with these powerful emotions.

FUTURE SCIENCE

Scientists are making new discoveries about the human body every day. In the future, there will be lots of different technologies available that will change the way humans medically treat their bodies forever.

If you are feeling sick and go to a doctor, they try to figure out what's wrong based on how you are feeling and what your body is doing. These are called **symptoms**. Doctors combine this information with knowledge about your family history to discover the problem. This is called a **diagnosis**.

COMPUTER AID

Doctors normally get it right, but sometimes getting an accurate diagnosis can be difficult. This is where computers can help. They can look at all your data, including millions of other patients, to come up with their own diagnoses to help the doctor.

SMARTER DRUGS

If you get sick, you are given the same medicine or drug as everyone else. But what if you could take a drug that was made to work better on you than on others? This is becoming a possibility.

Everyone's body is slightly different in very complex ways. In the future, doctors will be able to get the unique blueprint of each and every patient by reading their DNA through a technology called **gene sequencing**. A computer will be able to test which drugs work best with a particular patient's body, and prescribe those to them.

ROBOTIC CARE

When you get older, it's not as easy to move around and take care of yourself. In the future, you might have robots to help take care of you. They could clean your teeth, get you dressed and make you eggs on toast in the morning.

ROBO-SURGEONS

Surgery is performed by a special doctor called a surgeon when you need something fixed inside of your body. These days, it is likely to be **keyhole surgery**. This is where all of the surgical instruments go through a small hole in your skin and are remotely controlled by the surgeon, a bit like a computer game.

It is becoming possible for surgeons to perform remote-controlled operations on patients from huge distances. This is great because it means that vulnerable people can stay where they are and skilled surgeons can heal many people all over the world in the same day.

NANOBOTS

Further in the future, we might have robots that can perform surgeries inside your body. These tiny robotic **nanobots** would go into your body and detect and repair damaged tissue.

FUTURE SCIENCE

Some future technologies could change humankind in extraordinary ways. Let's take a closer look at what these technologies are and what they might mean for human life.

GROW YOUR OWN ORGANS

Currently, people with damaged organs have to wait for a **donor organ** from someone else. However, there is a shortage of donors, and even when an organ is available, their body's immune system might reject it.

In the future, it may be possible to make copies of your own organs in a laboratory using your stem cells. **Stem cells** are the very first cells that formed when you were a fertilized egg in your mother's womb. They are amazing because they can turn into any other cell in the body. Scientists could use them to grow new organs for people who need them.

RE-WRITING YOUR DNA

Some diseases are genetic, which means that they were in your DNA from birth. A new technology called **CRISPR** can edit your DNA by cutting out or replacing the parts that cause the disease.

Once this is fully understood, humans might one day be able to cure all diseases. A step beyond that would be to edit DNA to make people into super humans with greater strength and health.

RISE OF THE CYBORGS

One day, prosthetic limbs may become so good that they are just as effective as your own body and perhaps even better. As we get old, we might start replacing parts of ourselves with machines until we are cyborgs, half-human and half-robot!

A BRAIN IN A JAR?

Brains just need a flow of blood that is rich in oxygen and nutrients to survive, so maybe a brain could exist in a jar with a pipe feeding it fresh blood. You could possibly move your brain into other bodies, as long as you wired it up right!

Perhaps you don't need a brain at all! What if you could scan your entire brain and download all your personality, thoughts and emotions into a computer? Then, in the future, you could live in a robot body and fly off to explore the Universe.

HAIRLESS

Humans are similar to chimpanzees. Many thousands of years ago, you would have had long hair all over your body. You still have the same number of hairs on your body as a chimpanzee does, but most of your hair is now very short and thin.

HAIRY GROWTH

The hair on your head grows throughout your whole life, about three hundredths of an inch every three days. You lose about 50 to 100 hairs every day, but luckily these are replaced by new ones.

UNIQUE EAR WAX

Everyone's earwax is slightly different! It is a bit like a chemical fingerprint that scientists can use to figure out where a person's family is from.

MY DOG SMELLS GREAT!

Dogs have an amazing sense of smell! They have up to 300 million olfactory receptors, which is about 40 times more than humans have.

A GOOD STRETCH
You stretch out overnight, so when you wake up in the morning you are about one third of an inch taller than when you go to bed at night.
Hey guys, I hope I've been helpful!
Of course, Dominic! You've been a very useful guinea pig… uh, I mean human… helper.
Wow, you human beings really are a fascinating bunch! Although this is the end of our adventure, it is just the beginning of yours. There are even more amazing things for you to learn and many mysteries about the human body that we don't understand. Perhaps one day you will discover something incredible about the human body that you can share with the world.
Until next time, my biological marvels, goodbye, and don't forget: **KNOWLEDGE AWAITS!**
ASTRO LABS

GLOSSARY-INDEX

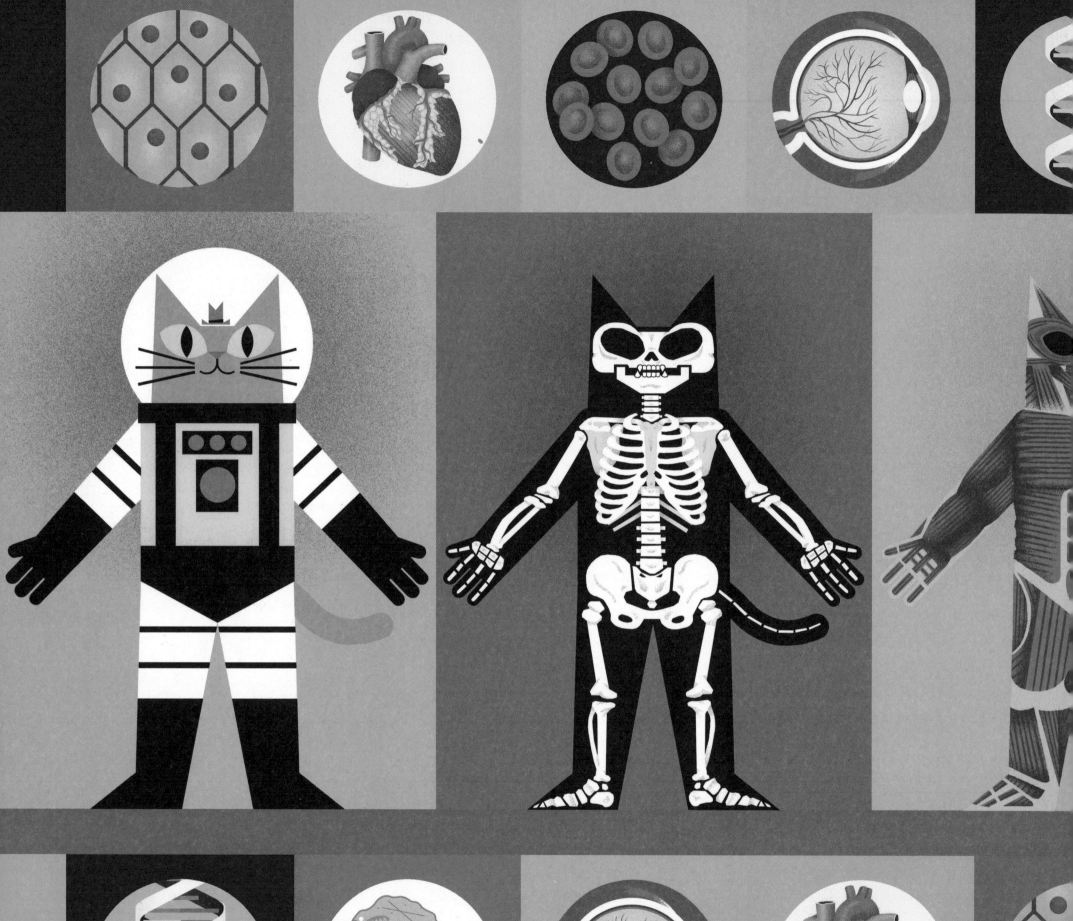